My Happiness TRACKER

A JOURNAL TO HELP YOU MAP OUT AND MANAGE YOUR HAPPINESS

ANNA BARNES

MY HAPPINESS TRACKER

Text by Amanda Nicholls

An Hachette UK Company
www.hachette.co.uk

Vie Books, an imprint of Summersdale Publishers Ltd
Part of Octopus Publishing Group Limited
Carmelite House
50 Victoria Embankment
LONDON
EC4Y 0DZ
UK

www.summersdale.com

Printed and bound in China

ISBN: 978-1-80007-446-0

Substantial discounts on bulk quantities of Summersdale books are available to corporations, professional associations and other organizations. For details contact general enquiries: telephone: +44 (0) 1243 771107 or email: enquiries@summersdale.com.

Disclaimer

This book is not intended as a substitute for the medical advice of a doctor or physician. If you are experiencing problems with your health, it is always best to follow the advice of a medical professional.

Introduction

Why track the elusive, intangible, shapeshifting beast that is happiness? Monitoring joy sounds a little counterintuitive, does it not?

Actually, awareness is the first step toward change, acceptance and contentment. Closely observing, measuring and jotting down our thoughts can help us really absorb them and maintain mindfulness and balance, especially with the amount of stuff competing for our attention these days. This book is for those looking to take an active role in cultivating growth, development and optimism by introducing happier thoughts into every day.

Within these pages, you'll find tips, tricks, tick lists and trackers for you to fill in, all bundled up in handy, bite-size, month-by-month packages to guide you through the year. Like taming an unruly yet beautiful horse, harnessing happiness can feel like a bit of a Herculean task,

so it helps to break it down into smaller component parts. Once you've completed a couple of months, you may be able to identify behavioural patterns you didn't realize were there and highlight daily habits and attitudes that could be affecting your mood.

When life gets overwhelming, it can be beneficial to map out what makes you smile and the positive impact it has on your day-to-day life. Take stock and make sure to track your happiness regularly to maximize your sense of fulfilment.

This book is not a manual as such; its mission is to be a useful companion for documenting and digesting your days, to nourish your mind and body and help you feel at your best.

Observe, learn and grow.

Wellness Tracker

On each day this month, colour in one shape
according to how you feel.

KEY ☐ Great ☐ Good ☐ Average
☐ Poor ☐ Terrible

It is only possible to live happily ever after on a day-to-day basis.

MARGARET WANDER BONANNO

Monthly Goals Tracker

Use this page to write down some of the things that you would like to achieve this month. Then think about ways you could accomplish them, and write down some ideas you could try.

My goal(s) for this month:

Example goal: Drink at least one litre of water a day

....

....

....

....

How I can reach them:

Example steps: Fill a water bottle every morning and keep it close by

....

....

....

....

Top Tips

JUST SAY YES

Here's a fun challenge: make yourself take every positive opportunity that comes your way for a week, a month or a year. Say yes to things that you would previously have disregarded as beyond your comfort zone, according to your established idea of yourself. Do something unexpected or out of character – perform at an open mic night, be the first to hit the dance floor at a party, shout at the top of your lungs at a local landmark. The outcome? Fresh learning experiences, new passions, hobbies, friends, contacts. Sometimes, the benefits of atypical encounters and introductions only show themselves years down the line, but often you can trace them back to these moments where you stepped outside your usual. This can be a particularly satisfying strategy after a life event that's left you reeling. Letting someone else lead or limiting our own adventures is an easy habit to fall into but don't forget how liberating it is to do things for yourself again, so book that skydive or try that new hairstyle without delay.

Self-Care Bucket List

It's important to include a few moments of self-care into every day. By trying just one of these simple self-care activities each week you will enrich your life and nourish your mind, body and soul.

Watch the
sunrise

Go for a brisk
lunchtime walk
or jog

Buy from
independent
stores

Put your phone
down for an hour
(baby steps!)

Water Tracker

One drop = one glass (400 ml)

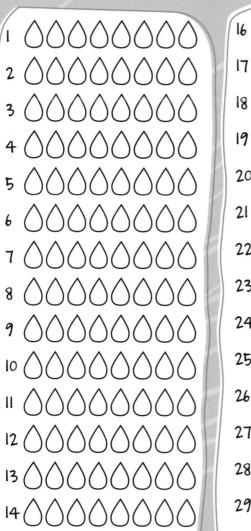

1	⬡⬡⬡⬡⬡⬡⬡⬡
2	⬡⬡⬡⬡⬡⬡⬡⬡
3	⬡⬡⬡⬡⬡⬡⬡⬡
4	⬡⬡⬡⬡⬡⬡⬡⬡
5	⬡⬡⬡⬡⬡⬡⬡⬡
6	⬡⬡⬡⬡⬡⬡⬡⬡
7	⬡⬡⬡⬡⬡⬡⬡⬡
8	⬡⬡⬡⬡⬡⬡⬡⬡
9	⬡⬡⬡⬡⬡⬡⬡⬡
10	⬡⬡⬡⬡⬡⬡⬡⬡
11	⬡⬡⬡⬡⬡⬡⬡⬡
12	⬡⬡⬡⬡⬡⬡⬡⬡
13	⬡⬡⬡⬡⬡⬡⬡⬡
14	⬡⬡⬡⬡⬡⬡⬡⬡
15	⬡⬡⬡⬡⬡⬡⬡⬡
16	⬡⬡⬡⬡⬡⬡⬡⬡
17	⬡⬡⬡⬡⬡⬡⬡⬡
18	⬡⬡⬡⬡⬡⬡⬡⬡
19	⬡⬡⬡⬡⬡⬡⬡⬡
20	⬡⬡⬡⬡⬡⬡⬡⬡
21	⬡⬡⬡⬡⬡⬡⬡⬡
22	⬡⬡⬡⬡⬡⬡⬡⬡
23	⬡⬡⬡⬡⬡⬡⬡⬡
24	⬡⬡⬡⬡⬡⬡⬡⬡
25	⬡⬡⬡⬡⬡⬡⬡⬡
26	⬡⬡⬡⬡⬡⬡⬡⬡
27	⬡⬡⬡⬡⬡⬡⬡⬡
28	⬡⬡⬡⬡⬡⬡⬡⬡
29	⬡⬡⬡⬡⬡⬡⬡⬡
30	⬡⬡⬡⬡⬡⬡⬡⬡
31	⬡⬡⬡⬡⬡⬡⬡⬡

Five-a-Day Tracker

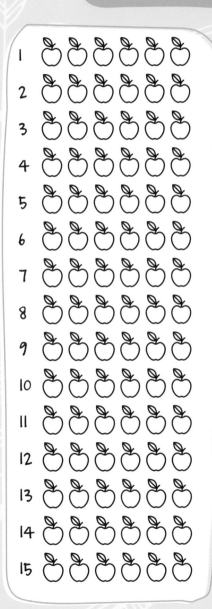

1
2
3
4
5
6
7
8
9
10
11
12
13
14
15

16
17
18
19
20
21
22
23
24
25
26
27
28
29
30
31

13

Sleep Tracker

On each day this month, colour in one shape according to how many hours of sleep you had.

KEY

- ◯ Four hours or fewer
- ◯ Five hours
- ◯ Six hours
- ◯ Seven hours
- ◯ Eight hours
- ◯ Nine hours or more

Top Tips

HAPPINESS COMES IN WAVES

The quiet splash of a good swim is up there with uninhibited hip swinging to your favourite song on the radio. These experiences pluck us from the whirlpool of our emotions and remind us of the here and now – guaranteed to help us switch off. You can't argue with endorphins.

Reaching stress saturation point? Immerse yourself in H_2O. There's merit in a relaxing bath – a hot soak does nicely – but a cold, preferably wild, dip clears the mind differently, and trains the attention. The focus on the physical leaves little room for anything else – there's nothing like it for gaining perspective and distracting from the daily grind.

The opportunity to concentrate on breathing is great for mind and body. Some health experts believe cold water therapy is a form of meditation that promotes positive mental health. Moreover, unless you're unusually committed to your phone and take it into the water in protective plastic (please, no), you're truly stepping away from your device, detaching from nagging notifications and allowing yourself to feel free.

Hibernate
and recharge
when you feel
the need

I'm grateful for...

Write one thing that you are grateful for each day this month.

2 3 4 5 6 7 8 9 10 11 12 13 14 15 16 17 18 19 20 21 22 23 24 25 26 27 28 29 30 31

Wellness Tracker

On each day this month, colour in one shape
according to how you feel.

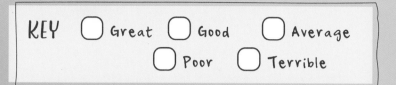

KEY ☐ Great ☐ Good ☐ Average
☐ Poor ☐ Terrible

To be content doesn't mean
you don't desire more,
it means you're thankful
for what you have and
patient for what's to come.

TONY GASKINS

Monthly Goals Tracker

Use this page to write down some of the things that you would like to achieve this month. Then think about ways you could accomplish them, and write down some ideas you could try.

My goal(s) for this month:

Example goal: Be kinder to myself

....

....

....

....

How I can reach them:

Example steps: Give myself at least three compliments throughout the day

....

....

....

....

Top Tips

YOU DO YOU

Being kind and considerate to others should be at the core of a contented daily existence, but going your own way is also key. Be sure to keep sight of and prioritize your wants and needs because – as the saying goes – you must put on your oxygen mask before you can help others with theirs. Remember you don't have to achieve something every day; we all move at different paces. Just being present here on this planet is a big deal and you should spend your waking moments the way that's right for you.

A timely reminder for this month, which for some can come loaded with pressure: whether you choose to celebrate or ignore Valentine's Day in its entirety, or perhaps go all-out for a "Palentine" instead, don't allow yourself to feel judged for your choice. Do whatever sparks joy.

Self-Care Bucket List

It's important to include a few moments of self-care into every day. By trying just one of these simple self-care activities each week you will enrich your life and nourish your mind, body and soul.

Prepare a stack of pancakes with your favourite toppings

Reach out to an old friend

Give yourself a little present

Download a bite-size language learning app

Water Tracker

One drop = one glass (400 ml)

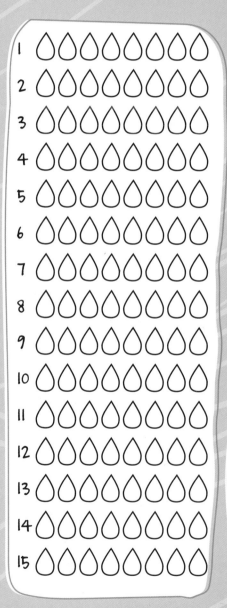

1	⬡⬡⬡⬡⬡⬡⬡⬡
2	⬡⬡⬡⬡⬡⬡⬡⬡
3	⬡⬡⬡⬡⬡⬡⬡⬡
4	⬡⬡⬡⬡⬡⬡⬡⬡
5	⬡⬡⬡⬡⬡⬡⬡⬡
6	⬡⬡⬡⬡⬡⬡⬡⬡
7	⬡⬡⬡⬡⬡⬡⬡⬡
8	⬡⬡⬡⬡⬡⬡⬡⬡
9	⬡⬡⬡⬡⬡⬡⬡⬡
10	⬡⬡⬡⬡⬡⬡⬡⬡
11	⬡⬡⬡⬡⬡⬡⬡⬡
12	⬡⬡⬡⬡⬡⬡⬡⬡
13	⬡⬡⬡⬡⬡⬡⬡⬡
14	⬡⬡⬡⬡⬡⬡⬡⬡
15	⬡⬡⬡⬡⬡⬡⬡⬡
16	⬡⬡⬡⬡⬡⬡⬡⬡
17	⬡⬡⬡⬡⬡⬡⬡⬡
18	⬡⬡⬡⬡⬡⬡⬡⬡
19	⬡⬡⬡⬡⬡⬡⬡⬡
20	⬡⬡⬡⬡⬡⬡⬡⬡
21	⬡⬡⬡⬡⬡⬡⬡⬡
22	⬡⬡⬡⬡⬡⬡⬡⬡
23	⬡⬡⬡⬡⬡⬡⬡⬡
24	⬡⬡⬡⬡⬡⬡⬡⬡
25	⬡⬡⬡⬡⬡⬡⬡⬡
26	⬡⬡⬡⬡⬡⬡⬡⬡
27	⬡⬡⬡⬡⬡⬡⬡⬡
28	⬡⬡⬡⬡⬡⬡⬡⬡
29	⬡⬡⬡⬡⬡⬡⬡⬡

Five-a-Day Tracker

Each apple = one of your five
fruits or vegetables a day

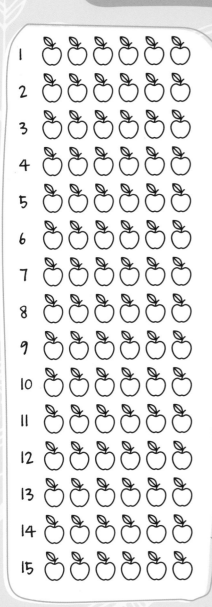

1
2
3
4
5
6
7
8
9
10
11
12
13
14
15

16
17
18
19
20
21
22
23
24
25
26
27
28
29

Sleep Tracker

On each day this month, colour in one shape according to how many hours of sleep you had.

KEY

- ◯ Four hours or fewer
- ◯ Five hours
- ◯ Six hours
- ◯ Seven hours
- ◯ Eight hours
- ◯ Nine hours or more

Top Tips

THE BRIDGET JONES EFFECT

Journalling is a creative outlet that can help you self-counsel and process the events that happen in your life. Research has found that writing about your feelings can assist in overcoming upset and leave you feeling happier. Brain scans on volunteers have shown that putting pen to paper reduces activity in the amygdala (the cerebral component regu-lating emotion intensity). In psychology, it is sometimes known as "the Bridget Jones effect" and it helps release feelings we might be reluctant to vocalize, whether it's a diary, a few lines of prose, poetry or lyrics.

It's hard to grow bored or lonely when you're your own pen pal; this also offers a chance to reconnect with your inner self and get to know your voice. What's more, with all the typing we do now, it's a nice way of keeping hold of the handwriting you spent so long honing at school. Whether it's abstract ideas or good/bad parts of your day, start by letting your thoughts flow for five minutes.

You are
worthy of
love and
happiness

I'm
grateful
for...

Write one thing
that you are
grateful for
each day
this month.

2 3 4 5 6 7 8 9 10 11 12 13 14 15 16 17 18 19 20 21 22 23 24 25 26 27 28 29

Wellness Tracker

On each day this month, colour in one shape
according to how you feel.

KEY
◻ Great ◻ Good ◻ Average
◻ Poor ◻ Terrible

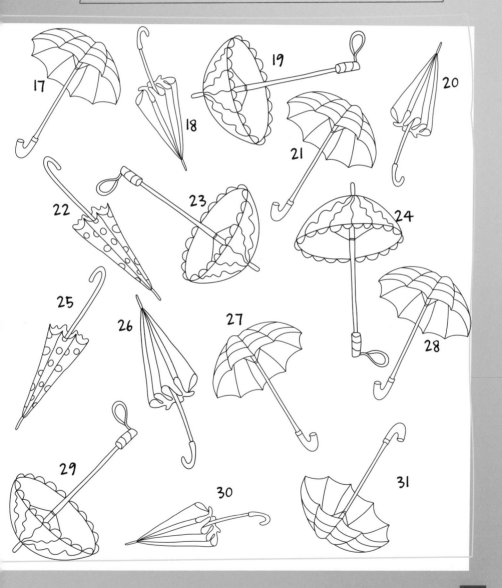

Breathe. Let go.
And remind yourself that
this very moment is the
only one you know you
have for sure.

OPRAH WINFREY

Monthly Goals Tracker

Use this page to write down some of the things that you would like to achieve this month. Then think about ways you could accomplish them, and write down some ideas you could try.

My goal(s) for this month:

Example goal: Make a nutritious meal most days of the week

....

....

....

How I can reach them:

Example steps: Create a meal plan, stock up on the ingredients and prep the day before

....

....

....

....

Top Tips

GROW YOUR OWN

There is such reward in harvesting your own food, and great joy in sharing the bounty with family and friends. Growing things in the garden is also a fun, achievement-oriented experience – the focus on learning and mastery can provide a real sense of satisfaction. Engaging in better environmental practices, surrounded by vibrant natural colours and fragrances, makes us feel good too, as do the accompanying fresh air and exercise. Furthermore, if you carefully cultivate your own fruit, flowers, herbs and veg, this removes any worries about what's in your food – you'll know better than anyone! Digging down and making contact with the earth has its benefits: soil is full of microbes, including mood-boosting *Mycobacterium vaccae*. This year, make a point of planting something you've never grown before or pick and dry your own seasonal bouquets – saving you money and not racking up a single air mile – and just wait for the compliments to roll in when you display them in your living space.

Self-Care Bucket List

It's important to include a few moments of self-care into every day. By trying just one of these simple self-care activities each week you will enrich your life and nourish your mind, body and soul.

Explore a local art trail

Try a new musical instrument or join a choir

Pen a letter instead of an email

Try a new fruit or vegetable - learn its origins and how to cook it

Water Tracker

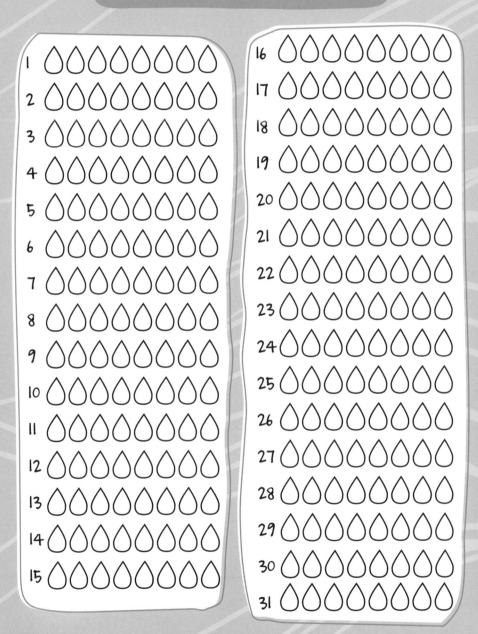

Five-a-Day Tracker

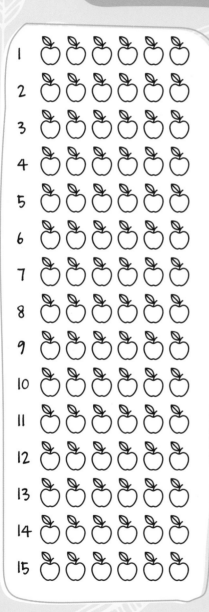

1
2
3
4
5
6
7
8
9
10
11
12
13
14
15

16
17
18
19
20
21
22
23
24
25
26
27
28
29
30
31

Sleep Tracker

On each day this month, colour in one shape according to how many hours of sleep you had.

KEY

- ◯ Four hours or fewer
- ◯ Five hours
- ◯ Six hours
- ◯ Seven hours
- ◯ Eight hours
- ◯ Nine hours or more

Top Tips

JUST SAY NO

While there's power in saying "yes", there's also strength in saying "no". It all comes down to context, and identifying what serves you. If you find yourself agreeing to everything as a people-pleasing exercise rather than a door-opening endeavour, you can quickly veer off-course.

Don't run yourself ragged trying not to disappoint. You don't need to be friends with everyone, nor is it possible to be. Being everywhere and everything to everyone will likely lead to physical and emotional exhaustion. There's freedom in accepting you won't be the whole world's cup of tea, and they won't be yours.

Embrace the JOMO (Joy of Missing Out). You probably don't need to attend your sister's boyfriend's cousin's baby shower. Nobody will think less of you. It's OK to sit out your sixth social engagement of the week; you don't need to send that huge essay text explaining why. A friend will understand.

Resist any
urge to change
yourself to
suit others

I'm grateful for...

Write one thing that you are grateful for each day this month.

1 2 3 4 5 6 7 8 9 10 11 12 13 14 15 16 17 18 19 20 21 22 23 24 25 26 27 28 29 30 31

Wellness Tracker

On each day this month, colour in one shape
according to how you feel.

The minute you
learn to love yourself,
you would not want
to be anyone else.

RIHANNA

Monthly Goals Tracker

Use this page to write down some of the things that you would like to achieve this month. Then think about ways you could accomplish them, and write down some ideas you could try.

My goal(s) for this month:

Example goal: Spend more time outside every day

....

....

....

....

How I can reach them:

Example steps: Pack a lunch or fill a flask to enjoy on my lunch breaks

....

....

....

....

Top Tips

RECHARGE IN NATURE

Studies looking at the connection between biodiversity and human health found that increasing the number of trees in a community and the availability of daily contact with nature resulted in a reduction in prescribed anti-depressants. Isn't that something?

And it's not just the visual aspectof going outdoors that's imp-ortant. It helps to stroll around your local green space without headphones or sunglasses, or anything obscuring the senses. For the most beneficial connection, all five should be engaged. Pause to run your fingers over rough bark, new growth or a tear in a tree. Taste the air, notice the rustling wind, the scent of freshly cut grass and flowers coming into bloom, or peaty soil, wet dog and decomposing leaves making your nose wrinkle.

Got a couple of hours? Try forest bathing (*shinrin yoku*) – the Japanese practice of being quiet among the trees. Turn off your devices, take long breaths into the abdomen, keep your eyes open and absorb the calming colours.

Self-Care Bucket List

It's important to include a few moments of self-care into every day. By trying just one of these simple self-care activities each week you will enrich your life and nourish your mind, body and soul.

Take old garments to a textile recycler or clothes bank ☐

Spring clean and declutter: tidy house, tidy mind ☐

Plan a dinner party for a few close friends ☐

Start a WhatsApp group for your street to foster community spirit ☐

Water Tracker

One drop = one glass (400 ml)

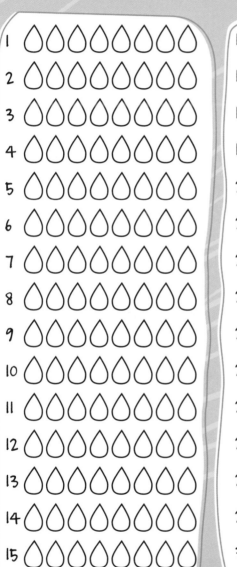

1
2
3
4
5
6
7
8
9
10
11
12
13
14
15
16
17
18
19
20
21
22
23
24
25
26
27
28
29
30

Five-a-Day Tracker

Each apple = one of your five
fruits or vegetables a day

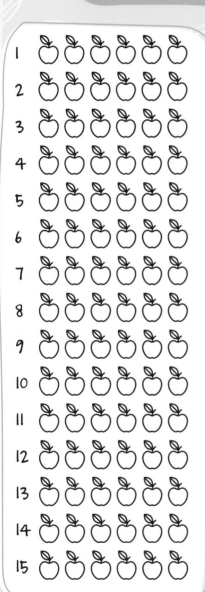

1	16
2	17
3	18
4	19
5	20
6	21
7	22
8	23
9	24
10	25
11	26
12	27
13	28
14	29
15	30

Sleep Tracker

On each day this month, colour in one shape according to how many hours of sleep you had.

KEY

- Four hours or fewer
- Five hours
- Six hours
- Seven hours
- Eight hours
- Nine hours or more

Top Tips

REFRAME YOUR FLAWS

Encourage change in yourself and be willing to evolve, but recognize how difficult some things are to alter, especially behaviours learned in our early years. This doesn't mean we shouldn't try to improve unhelpful habits, but that we also have the choice to accept rather than chastise ourselves, and see traits we consider flaws differently – to reframe them.

It's unfortunate to have been through difficulties, especially if they have changed us in a way we wouldn't have chosen, but we can try to focus on the lessons these experiences may have instilled. Certain things are easier to reframe than others, but adopting this mindset can prove useful.

Embrace your quirks, and the one-off nature of your experience on Earth, rather than constantly apologizing for who you are. Everything that has happened to you – good and bad – has contributed to your unique perspective on the world. When we feel free enough to be completely ourselves, happiness usually follows.

Never measure
your own
happiness by
other people's
definition of it

I'm grateful for...

Write one thing that you are grateful for each day this month.

2 3 4 5 6 7 8 9 10 11 12 13 14 15 16 17 18 19 20 21 22 23 24 25 26 27 28 29 30

Seeing my friends.
playing kahoot
Going Swimming

Wellness Tracker

On each day this month, colour in one shape
according to how you feel.

*It is the ultimate luxury
to combine passion and
contribution. It's also a
very clear path to happiness.*

SHERYL SANDBERG

Monthly Goals Tracker

Use this page to write down some of the things that you would like to achieve this month. Then think about ways you could accomplish them, and write down some ideas you could try.

My goal(s) for this month:

Example goal: Spend time on a particular goal that I'm working toward

....

....

....

How I can reach them:

Example steps: Create a mood board of images, clippings and quotes

....

....

....

....

Top Tips

THE CAREER MYTH

Years ago, people worked to buy food and clothes for their family. Nowadays, it's all about the professional pathway – "making something of yourself" and "having it all". Society can seem to suggest that if we aren't studying, furthering a fabulous career or having children, we're failing. In the same way that bringing up kids isn't for everyone, we're not all naturally academic or career-minded. Stressed about where you're headed? Try to reframe the uncertainties of the future as a landscape of undiscovered opportunities, and remember there's nothing wrong with simply putting your hours in to live a life that's enjoyable for you.

That said, in terms of daily happiness, most of us spend lots of time working or studying, so make sure your conditions are good and you're contributing to something you care about, if you can. Passion and purpose breed motivation and joy. Is there time to volunteer for a cause you feel strongly about? Helping others can have a feel-good effect and help us see things with fresh eyes while we make a real difference.

Self-Care Bucket List

It's important to include a few moments of self-care into every day. By trying just one of these simple self-care activities each week you will enrich your life and nourish your mind, body and soul.

Explore parts of the local area you've never been to

Meal prep for the week so you know you'll eat well

Revive a vintage field game such as ring toss or skittles

Make a list of road trips you'd like to do

Water Tracker

One drop = one glass (400 ml)

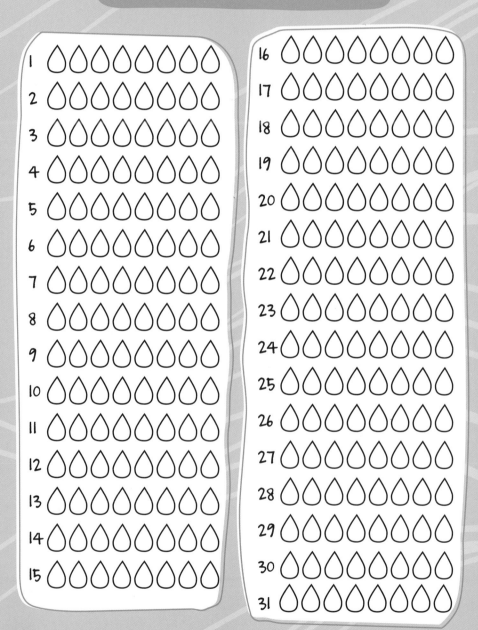

Five-a-Day Tracker

Each apple = one of your five fruits or vegetables a day

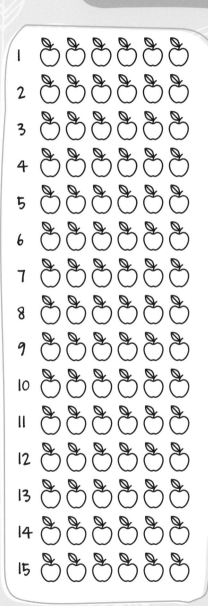

1
2
3
4
5
6
7
8
9
10
11
12
13
14
15

16
17
18
19
20
21
22
23
24
25
26
27
28
29
30
31

Sleep Tracker

On each day this month, colour in one shape according to how many hours of sleep you had.

KEY

- ◯ Four hours or fewer
- ◯ Five hours
- ◯ Six hours
- ◯ Seven hours
- ◯ Eight hours
- ◯ Nine hours or more

Top Tips

GO SOLO

It's important to distinguish loneliness – proven to be detrimental to well-being – from alone time, which can be healthy, liberating and happiness-conducive. The idea of going for dinner alone would horrify some as it goes against the grain of social norms, but it's nothing to be afraid of. The more we do these things, the more they normalize. Solitude can increase empathy, creativity, productivity and mental strength. Studies link tolerance of alone time to better life satisfaction, improved stress management and less depression. It can make you appreciate social occasions more and decrease your need for validation – and the busier you are, the more you'll benefit.

Read in a café. Plan a trip alone. Take yourself to the cinema. Don't avoid time with your thoughts. This nourishes the soul, builds confidence and helps you recalibrate. Whatever it is you choose, try to make time to be with yourself every day and process the events of the previous 24 hours to avoid overwhelm.

Every day
contains a
reason
to smile

I'm grateful for...

Write one thing that you are grateful for each day this month.

Wellness Tracker

On each day this month, colour in one shape
according to how you feel.

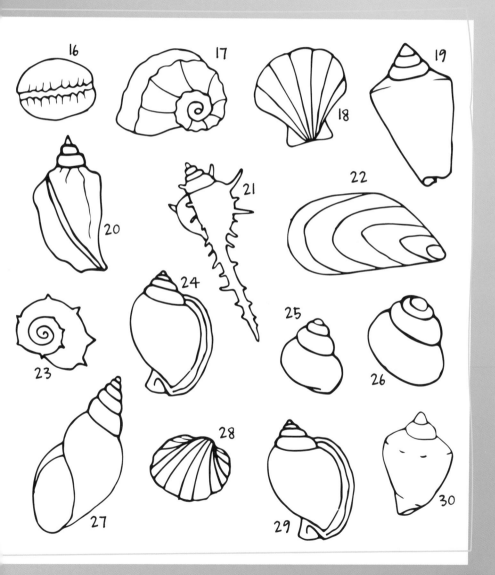

Accept no one's
definition of your life;
define yourself.

HARVEY FIERSTEIN

Monthly
Goals Tracker

Use this page to write down some of the things that you would like to achieve this month. Then think about ways you could accomplish them, and write down some ideas you could try.

My goal(s) for this month:

Example goal: Drink less caffeine throughout the day

....

....

....

....

How I can reach them:

Example steps: Limit myself to one tea/coffee a day and buy decaffeinated options

....

....

....

....

Top Tips

QUIT THE COMPARISON CLUB

If you're prone to lapping up the shiny-looking lives on social media and getting sucked into a virtual vortex of comparison that chips away at your self-esteem, limiting your screen time is paramount in optimizing your happiness in real life. Comparison culture can be damaging, so, when you can, put your phone down for the day; maybe even take a week or month away from social media.

Take a photo of something beautiful that you've seen or done and *don't* share it with a single soul. Savour the feeling that this is something just for you, that nobody needs to know about. You do not require approval for your tastes, choices or lifestyle. At the start, it's hard to stop your fingers absent-mindedly opening any offending apps (delete them completely if the temptation is too much), but make an effort to resist the urge and you'll be weaned off before you know it, and wondering what you saw in them in the first place.

Self-Care Bucket List

It's important to include a few moments of self-care into every day. By trying just one of these simple self-care activities each week you will enrich your life and nourish your mind, body and soul.

Sketch, paint or stargaze outdoors

Have a picnic or barbecue in the park

Plan outfits for the week to avoid morning stress

Shout a truth from the proverbial rooftops

Water Tracker

One drop = one glass (400 ml)

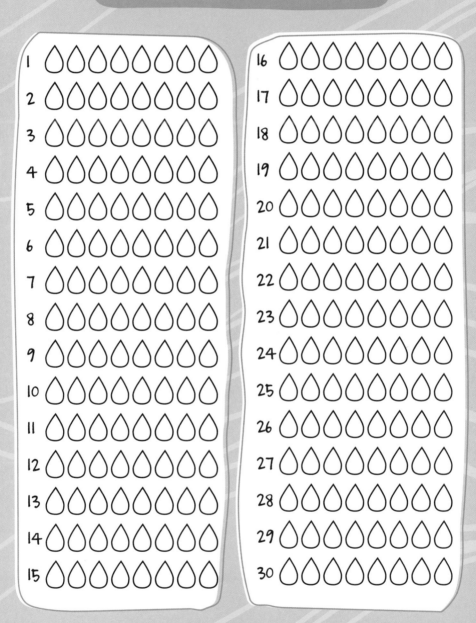

Five-a-Day Tracker

Each apple = one of your five
fruits or vegetables a day

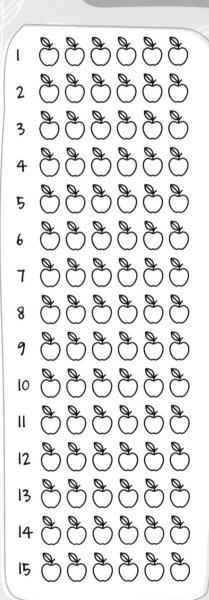

1	16
2	17
3	18
4	19
5	20
6	21
7	22
8	23
9	24
10	25
11	26
12	27
13	28
14	29
15	30

Sleep Tracker

On each day this month, colour in one shape according to how many hours of sleep you had.

KEY

- ⚪ Four hours or fewer
- ⚪ Five hours
- ⚪ Six hours
- ⚪ Seven hours
- ⚪ Eight hours
- ⚪ Nine hours or more

Top Tips

DISH OUT THE TO-DOS

Many of us live by the motto "if you want a job done well, do it yourself", convinced we cannot delegate. This can lead to burnout if we apply it to everything, every day. Relinquishing control is challenging, but what's the worst that can happen? Often, it's nothing disastrous. Those you delegate to may even surprise you when given the chance to step up and share responsibility, which may contribute to their sense of purpose, foster trust and deepen interpersonal connection.

Delegation is essential, and constant, in society – from our morning coffee, using beans we didn't grow, to putting on our pyjamas, which we sure didn't sew. It brings us all closer, and community – the feeling of belonging – is key to contentment. We all lean on each other's skills and have a role in making the world go round. Often, a day simply contains too many tasks for its 24 hours; accepting help is one of life's necessities.

We have a hand
in our own
happiness

I'm grateful for...

Write one thing that you are grateful for each day this month.

2 3 4 5 6 7 8 9 10 11 12 13 14 15 16 17 18 19 20 21 22 23 24 25 26 27 28 29 30

77

Wellness Tracker

On each day this month, colour in one shape
according to how you feel.

KEY ◯ Great ◯ Good ◯ Average ◯ Poor ◯ Terrible

*Happiness is
a direction,
not a place.*

SYDNEY J. HARRIS

Monthly
Goals Tracker

Use this page to write down some of the things that you would like to achieve this month. Then think about ways you could accomplish them, and write down some ideas you could try.

My goal(s) for this month:

Example goal: Cut back on social media and internet use

....

....

....

....

How I can reach them:

Example steps: Disable notifications and
set a screen time limit

....

....

....

....

Top Tips

TRAIN YOUR BRAIN

It's possible to elevate your basic happiness level using certain techniques. Our grey matter (the outermost layer of the brain that controls emotions) is capable of neuroplasticity (the ability to change through growth) and lifestyle and behaviour are big influences on its development throughout our lives. Practised regularly, the process of meditation – free to all – is believed to rewire brain regions, regulate how we experience our environment, reduce stress and increase clarity. If you diligently exercise your mindfulness muscle, you can reshape your thinking and create new behavioural pathways.

Set aside a few minutes each morning. With mental exercise, as with regular workouts, commitment and consistency matter more than duration. Make sure you're in a comfortable position, feel your breath, register other sounds, how your body feels and any emotion it's experiencing. Accept that your mind will wander – simply return it to focusing on your breath without judgement. Build to 30 minutes every day – if you manage eight weeks you'll have thickened your pre-frontal cortex, which helps with awareness, concentration, self-control, emotions and decision-making.

Self-Care Bucket List

It's important to include a few moments of self-care into every day. By trying just one of these simple self-care activities each week you will enrich your life and nourish your mind, body and soul.

Book a long weekend away

Take yourself on a date

Do 20 squats a day

Play a racket sport

Water Tracker

One drop = one glass (400 ml)

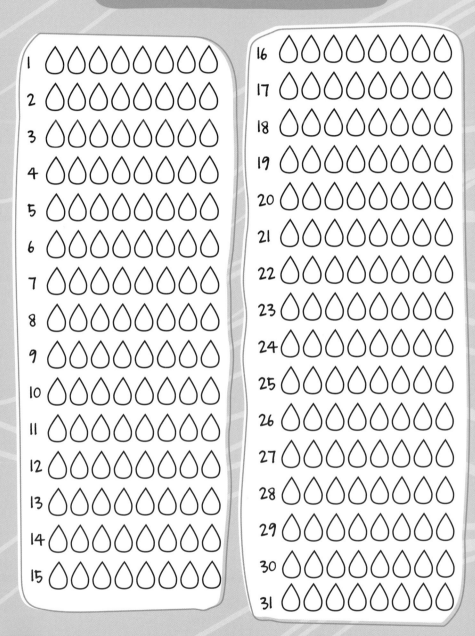

Five-a-Day Tracker

Each apple = one of your five
fruits or vegetables a day

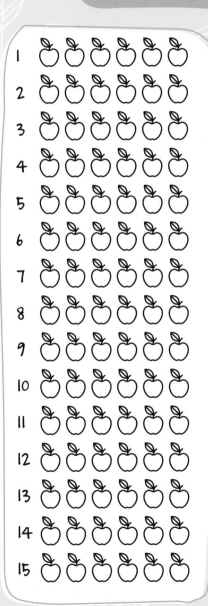

1
2
3
4
5
6
7
8
9
10
11
12
13
14
15

16
17
18
19
20
21
22
23
24
25
26
27
28
29
30
31

Sleep Tracker

On each day this month, colour in one shape according to how many hours of sleep you had.

KEY

- ☐ Four hours or fewer
- ☐ Five hours
- ☐ Six hours
- ☐ Seven hours
- ☐ Eight hours
- ☐ Nine hours or more

Top Tips

PROMOTE THE WIND-DOWN PROCESS

Never underestimate the import-ance of quality sleep for a happy mind and body. Niggly little things we'd normally barely bat an eyelid at can be blown up into something big, bad and bothersome by a tired brain. Each of us is different when it comes to functioning at our best, but generally, and ideally, we're looking at seven to nine hours every night, in a dark, quiet and well-ventilated room.

It's no secret that doom-scrolling on your smart device in the dark is a big no-no before bed, no matter how desperately you need to catch up on life admin. The blue light emitted by a smartphone or laptop messes up our 24-hour circadian rhythm (part of our internal body clock) and confuses the brain into thinking it's time to rise and shine rather than slip into the land of nod. Give yourself a good half-hour phone-free before bed – instead read, write, bathe or light a candle to promote the wind-down process.

Surround
yourself
with things
that bring
you joy

I'm grateful for...

Write one thing that you are grateful for each day this month.

1 2 3 4 5 6 7 8 9 10 11 12 13 14 15 16 17 18 19 20 21 22 23 24 25 26 27 28 29 30 31

Wellness Tracker

On each day this month, colour in one shape
according to how you feel.

KEY ☐ Great ☐ Good ☐ Average
☐ Poor ☐ Terrible

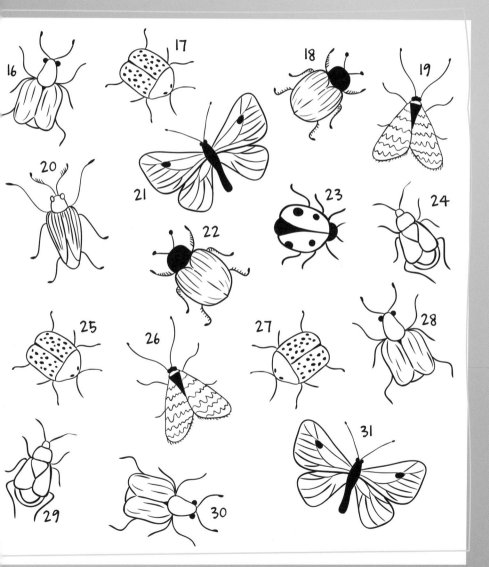

Happiness is not a goal...
It is a by-product of
a life well lived.

ELEANOR ROOSEVELT

Monthly Goals Tracker

Use this page to write down some of the things that you would like to achieve this month. Then think about ways you could accomplish them, and write down some ideas you could try.

My goal(s) for this month:

Example goal: Try a new activity or develop a hobby

....

....

....

....

How I can reach them:

Example steps: Research local groups or classes, or find online tutorials

....

....

....

....

Top Tips

PROJECT PASSION

Do more of what you love. No, not later... Now! So much of our life is taken up with the things we have to do – work, chores, admin – that carving out time to focus on what really inspires us is imperative. If you have a hobby or passion that's getting side-lined, schedule it like you would a meeting or appointment.

Pick up long-abandoned but once-loved activities again. Never been one for clubs and classes? Spend some time thinking about what excites you. Make more space for your friends, nurture meaningful relationships, read, get a massage, write a song, make your favourite cocktail, try cooking a different world cuisine, knit, sew, learn ceramics, make something with your hands, seek out live music and dance until you drop.

Create a "joy jar" to remember the month's happiest, most laughter-filled moments if you find yourself having a dip in mood. You might be surprised by how much happiness you already have in your life.

Self-Care Bucket List

It's important to include a few moments of self-care into every day. By trying just one of these simple self-care activities each week you will enrich your life and nourish your mind, body and soul.

Donate to a food bank

Stretch or do some yoga

Make a fresh, healthy meal from scratch

Run a bath with Epsom salts

Water Tracker

One drop = one glass (400 ml)

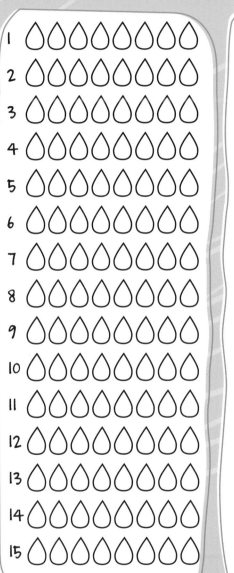

1 ◇◇◇◇◇◇◇◇
2 ◇◇◇◇◇◇◇◇
3 ◇◇◇◇◇◇◇◇
4 ◇◇◇◇◇◇◇◇
5 ◇◇◇◇◇◇◇◇
6 ◇◇◇◇◇◇◇◇
7 ◇◇◇◇◇◇◇◇
8 ◇◇◇◇◇◇◇◇
9 ◇◇◇◇◇◇◇◇
10 ◇◇◇◇◇◇◇◇
11 ◇◇◇◇◇◇◇◇
12 ◇◇◇◇◇◇◇◇
13 ◇◇◇◇◇◇◇◇
14 ◇◇◇◇◇◇◇◇
15 ◇◇◇◇◇◇◇◇

16 ◇◇◇◇◇◇◇◇
17 ◇◇◇◇◇◇◇◇
18 ◇◇◇◇◇◇◇◇
19 ◇◇◇◇◇◇◇◇
20 ◇◇◇◇◇◇◇◇
21 ◇◇◇◇◇◇◇◇
22 ◇◇◇◇◇◇◇◇
23 ◇◇◇◇◇◇◇◇
24 ◇◇◇◇◇◇◇◇
25 ◇◇◇◇◇◇◇◇
26 ◇◇◇◇◇◇◇◇
27 ◇◇◇◇◇◇◇◇
28 ◇◇◇◇◇◇◇◇
29 ◇◇◇◇◇◇◇◇
30 ◇◇◇◇◇◇◇◇
31 ◇◇◇◇◇◇◇◇

Five-a-Day Tracker

Each apple = one of your five
fruits or vegetables a day

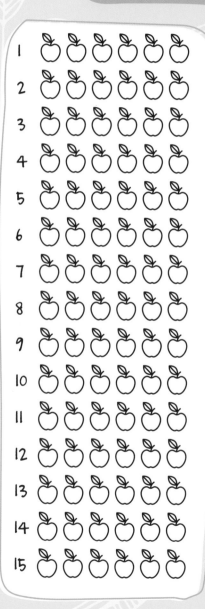

1
2
3
4
5
6
7
8
9
10
11
12
13
14
15

16
17
18
19
20
21
22
23
24
25
26
27
28
29
30
31

Sleep Tracker

On each day this month, colour in one shape according to how many hours of sleep you had.

KEY

- ◯ Four hours or fewer
- ◯ Five hours
- ◯ Six hours
- ◯ Seven hours
- ◯ Eight hours
- ◯ Nine hours or more

Top Tips

EXPRESS YOURSELF

Have faith in your own convictions, wisdoms and decisions. Everything you have done has been for a reason. Say what's on your mind, and if that's difficult, research and practise assertiveness training techniques, which are based on the principle that we all have a right to express our thoughts and feelings in a respectful way. When we don't feel we can express ourselves, depression, anxiety or anger can ensue and self-worth suffers.

This same reasoning applies to everyone, including those who frustrate us. Keeping this in mind can help us approach conflict with more calm. When people behave inexplicably it can usually be traced back to something that has happened to them – many negative behaviours stem from fear.

Try expressing your position on paper, then the opposing perspective. Sometimes there can be more than one kind of logic, and when it comes to emotional responses, often logic doesn't come into it at all. Be open to other points of view. Try to understand where someone is coming from, and how they arrived at this conclusion, and do your bit to promote unity, empathy and compassion.

Just like
with dessert,
there is always
room for fun

I'm grateful for...

Write one thing that you are grateful for each day this month.

Wellness Tracker

On each day this month, colour in one shape
according to how you feel.

KEY ◯ Great ◯ Good ◯ Average ◯ Poor ◯ Terrible

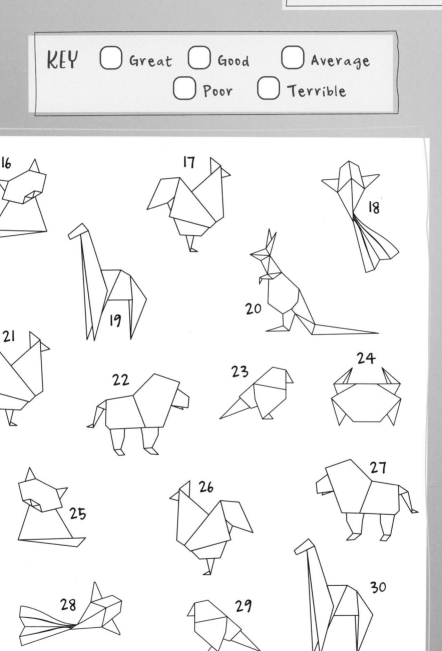

Joy comes to us in moments —
ordinary moments.
We risk missing out on joy
when we get too busy chasing
down the extraordinary.

BRENÉ BROWN

Monthly Goals Tracker

Use this page to write down some of the things that you would like to achieve this month. Then think about ways you could accomplish them, and write down some ideas you could try.

My goal(s) for this month:

Example goal: Try to cut my spending

....

....

....

....

How I can reach them:

Example steps: Create a spreadsheet to keep track of monthly expenditure

....

....

....

....

Top Tips

HAPPY STARTS AT HOME

We're spending more time than ever before in our humble abodes, with remote working having transformed the nature of the daily grind for many. When it comes to contentment, the importance of our immediate environment bears emphasizing. Why not take some time to freshen up your living space, with a straightforward lick of paint, a cabinet reshuffle, a new piece of art, some feng shui, or a cosy new blanket for snuggling under?

Gather up some produce – a basket of home-grown stone fruit or just-picked berries from local woodland, for instance – and fill the kitchen with rich, sweet fragrances while you meditatively make up jars of jam, or perhaps a pie. Allocate a new corner for crafting, or cocktail-making.

Reorganize your bedroom to give it a fresher feel, and initiate a wardrobe changeover (find your new go-to feel-good outfit while you're at it). A clear-out is always satisfying too; but be sure to check those old coat pockets – there's almost always coinage to be found, or a long-lost accessory…

Self-Care Bucket List

It's important to include a few moments of self-care into every day. By trying just one of these simple self-care activities each week you will enrich your life and nourish your mind, body and soul.

Make a life admin list (it's half the battle)

Find some local gardens to explore

Research your personality type and how to nourish its needs

Listen to a podcast or create an empowering playlist

Water Tracker

One drop = one glass (400 ml)

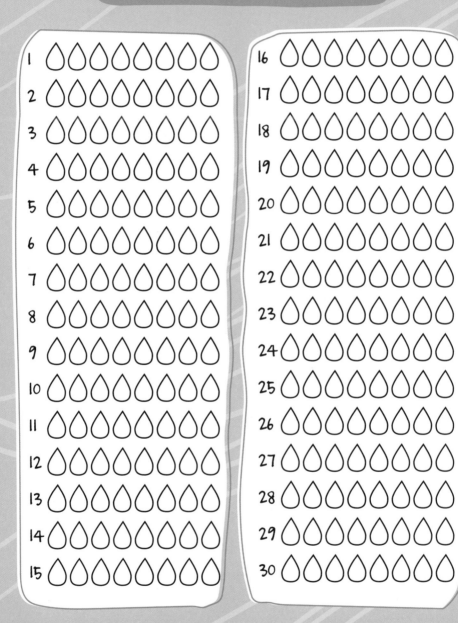

Five-a-Day Tracker

Each apple = one of your five
fruits or vegetables a day

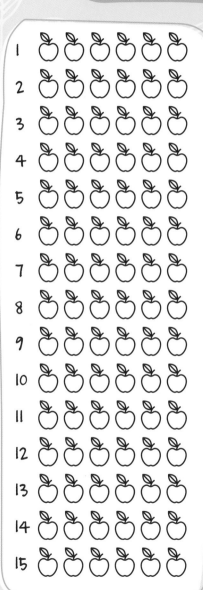

1 🍎🍎🍎🍎🍎🍎
2 🍎🍎🍎🍎🍎🍎
3 🍎🍎🍎🍎🍎🍎
4 🍎🍎🍎🍎🍎🍎
5 🍎🍎🍎🍎🍎🍎
6 🍎🍎🍎🍎🍎🍎
7 🍎🍎🍎🍎🍎🍎
8 🍎🍎🍎🍎🍎🍎
9 🍎🍎🍎🍎🍎🍎
10 🍎🍎🍎🍎🍎🍎
11 🍎🍎🍎🍎🍎🍎
12 🍎🍎🍎🍎🍎🍎
13 🍎🍎🍎🍎🍎🍎
14 🍎🍎🍎🍎🍎🍎
15 🍎🍎🍎🍎🍎🍎

16 🍎🍎🍎🍎🍎🍎
17 🍎🍎🍎🍎🍎🍎
18 🍎🍎🍎🍎🍎🍎
19 🍎🍎🍎🍎🍎🍎
20 🍎🍎🍎🍎🍎🍎
21 🍎🍎🍎🍎🍎🍎
22 🍎🍎🍎🍎🍎🍎
23 🍎🍎🍎🍎🍎🍎
24 🍎🍎🍎🍎🍎🍎
25 🍎🍎🍎🍎🍎🍎
26 🍎🍎🍎🍎🍎🍎
27 🍎🍎🍎🍎🍎🍎
28 🍎🍎🍎🍎🍎🍎
29 🍎🍎🍎🍎🍎🍎
30 🍎🍎🍎🍎🍎🍎

Sleep Tracker

On each day this month, colour in one shape according to how many hours of sleep you had.

KEY

- ◯ Four hours or fewer
- ◯ Five hours
- ◯ Six hours
- ◯ Seven hours
- ◯ Eight hours
- ◯ Nine hours or more

Top Tips

FIND YOUR TRIBE

Heard the saying: misery loves company? It refers to people who prefer their pals glum because fellow sufferers make unhappiness easier to bear. If there are people in your life who stir up negative thoughts when you hang out; who drain you and subtly dissuade you from taking positive steps or making proactive efforts, cut down the time you spend with them.

If someone wishes only to wallow with you, they make it harder to be happy, hopeful and productive. Similarly, while banter can be fun in a friendship, if playful joshing becomes barely disguised bullying, or your successes are played down rather than celebrated, this is likely an envious, insecure soul trying to make themselves feel better. By all means, tell them how you feel and give them a chance to change their ways, but trust your gut; know your worth.

Surround yourself with people who support you, toast your triumphs and appreciate your views, background, experiences and interests, even if they are not the same as theirs.

It's OK to
distance yourself
from something
that no longer
serves you
positively

I'm grateful for...

Write one thing that you are grateful for each day this month.

Wellness Tracker

On each day this month, colour in one shape
according to how you feel.

KEY ☐ Great ☐ Good ☐ Average ☐ Poor ☐ Terrible

*Being happy never
goes out of style.*

LILLY PULITZER

Monthly Goals Tracker

Use this page to write down some of the things that you would like to achieve this month. Then think about ways you could accomplish them, and write down some ideas you could try.

My goal(s) for this month:

Example goal: Sleep for eight hours a night

....

....

....

....

How I can reach them:

Example steps: Set a reminder to switch my phone off an hour before bedtime

....

....

....

....

Top Tips

#GOALS

Make a list of five things you didn't have, or hadn't achieved, five years ago, that you have now. This short, simple exercise can reassure you how much things evolve and, if you're feeling stuck in a life rut, remind you that just as much will have changed in the next few years – whether you intend it to or not. The one constant we have in life is change, and we can never predict what sort of opportunities might fall into our laps next.

Make a list or mood board for your future goals. If you draw them, this exercise can double up as a great form of art therapy. Each branch of a tree could represent a different area of your life that you'd like to tackle next. A garden with flourishing flower beds could signify what's going well and remind you of what you're grateful for.

Self-Care Bucket List

It's important to include a few moments of self-care into every day. By trying just one of these simple self-care activities each week you will enrich your life and nourish your mind, body and soul.

Avoid world news for the day

Watch funny videos online

Repair an item of clothing yourself

Carve a pumpkin and make zero-waste soup with the leftovers

Water Tracker

One drop = one glass (400 ml)

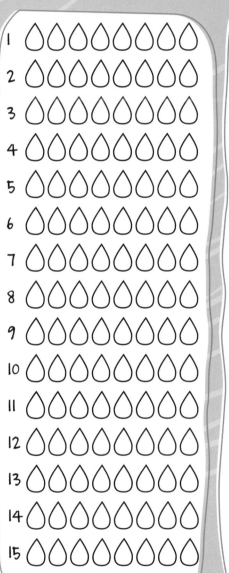

1 ⬭⬭⬭⬭⬭⬭⬭	16 ⬭⬭⬭⬭⬭⬭⬭
2 ⬭⬭⬭⬭⬭⬭⬭	17 ⬭⬭⬭⬭⬭⬭⬭
3 ⬭⬭⬭⬭⬭⬭⬭	18 ⬭⬭⬭⬭⬭⬭⬭
4 ⬭⬭⬭⬭⬭⬭⬭	19 ⬭⬭⬭⬭⬭⬭⬭
5 ⬭⬭⬭⬭⬭⬭⬭	20 ⬭⬭⬭⬭⬭⬭⬭
6 ⬭⬭⬭⬭⬭⬭⬭	21 ⬭⬭⬭⬭⬭⬭⬭
7 ⬭⬭⬭⬭⬭⬭⬭	22 ⬭⬭⬭⬭⬭⬭⬭
8 ⬭⬭⬭⬭⬭⬭⬭	23 ⬭⬭⬭⬭⬭⬭⬭
9 ⬭⬭⬭⬭⬭⬭⬭	24 ⬭⬭⬭⬭⬭⬭⬭
10 ⬭⬭⬭⬭⬭⬭⬭	25 ⬭⬭⬭⬭⬭⬭⬭
11 ⬭⬭⬭⬭⬭⬭⬭	26 ⬭⬭⬭⬭⬭⬭⬭
12 ⬭⬭⬭⬭⬭⬭⬭	27 ⬭⬭⬭⬭⬭⬭⬭
13 ⬭⬭⬭⬭⬭⬭⬭	28 ⬭⬭⬭⬭⬭⬭⬭
14 ⬭⬭⬭⬭⬭⬭⬭	29 ⬭⬭⬭⬭⬭⬭⬭
15 ⬭⬭⬭⬭⬭⬭⬭	30 ⬭⬭⬭⬭⬭⬭⬭
	31 ⬭⬭⬭⬭⬭⬭⬭

Five-a-Day Tracker

Each apple = one of your five fruits or vegetables a day

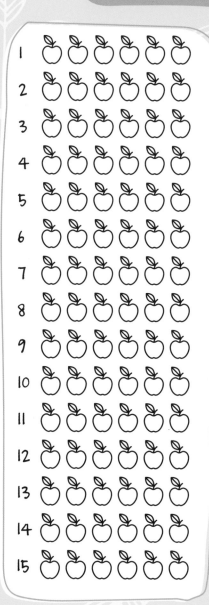

1
2
3
4
5
6
7
8
9
10
11
12
13
14
15

16
17
18
19
20
21
22
23
24
25
26
27
28
29
30
31

Sleep Tracker

On each day this month, colour in one shape according to how many hours of sleep you had.

KEY

- ◯ Four hours or fewer
- ◯ Five hours
- ◯ Six hours
- ◯ Seven hours
- ◯ Eight hours
- ◯ Nine hours or more

Top Tips

DON'T SILVER-LINE IT

The concept of a silver lining – a positive aspect to a negative situation – is age-old. We're very used to searching for these small comforts, even in the most awful circumstances, in hopes of making ourselves feel better or offering solace when we're not sure how to console. It's a conditioned response – our preoccupation with trying to fix things – but the notion of simply recognizing a bad situation is now being promoted, with studies finding that "cognitive reappraisal" (seeking a cheery spin) isn't always healthy.

It's important to feel "seen" by others, to know it is your right to be sad or upset, and grant yourself time to feel this way when something unpleasant occurs – rather than being encouraged to buck up because your lot isn't half as bad as someone else's. Finding the bright side in the face of an unlucky flat tyre is one thing, but it can be beneficial to fully feel the consequences of some negative events, and learn from them.

Self-care is
not a luxury,
it is a necessity

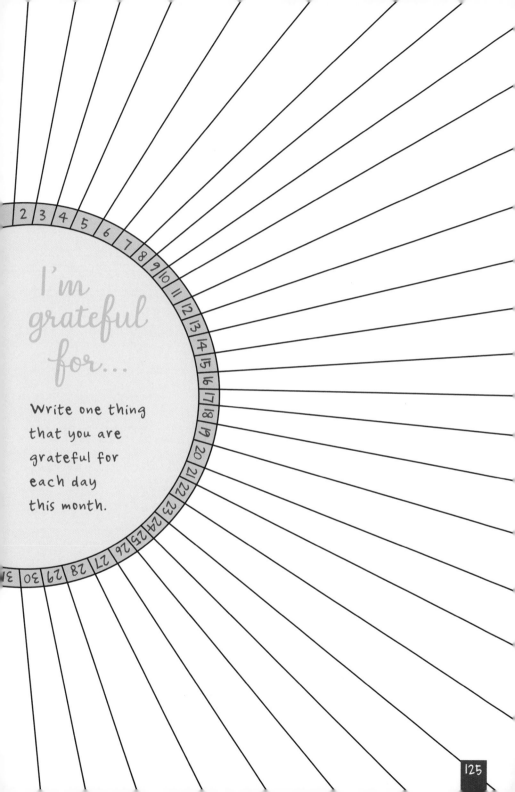

I'm grateful for...

Write one thing that you are grateful for each day this month.

2 3 4 5 6 7 8 9 10 11 12 13 14 15 16 17 18 19 20 21 22 23 24 25 26 27 28 29 30 31

Wellness Tracker

On each day this month, colour in one shape
according to how you feel.

KEY ◯ Great ◯ Good ◯ Average
◯ Poor ◯ Terrible

Happiness, not in another
place but this place,
not for another hour
but this hour.

WALT WHITMAN

Monthly
Goals Tracker

Use this page to write down some of the things that you would like to achieve this month. Then think about ways you could accomplish them, and write down some ideas you could try.

My goal(s) for this month:

Example goal: Meditate for at least five minutes a day

....

....

....

....

How I can reach them:

Example steps: Download a meditation app and start a beginner class

....

....

....

....

Top Tips

THE KINDNESS OF A STRANGER

When you wake up, rather than making a beeline for the mundane tasks of the day, take a moment to be still, thankful that you have another day ahead of you, and decide on something nice to do for yourself. Then, think up a few ideas around how you could have a positive impact on the other people you might encounter over the next 12 hours.

An act of kindness can lighten your own mood as well as make someone else's day – potentially restore their faith in the world, even. Look for chances to make a difference, from holding a door open for someone, saying good morning to those you pass on your daily stroll or offering a shoulder to cry on, to leaving a glowing review for a business you've been impressed by, or sending a care package to someone you know who's struggling.

Self-Care Bucket List

It's important to include a few moments of self-care into every day. By trying just one of these simple self-care activities each week you will enrich your life and nourish your mind, body and soul.

Binge that big new series

Treat yourself to a fancy face mask

Repeat a positive morning mantra

Check in with a long-distance relative

Water Tracker

One drop = one glass (400 ml)

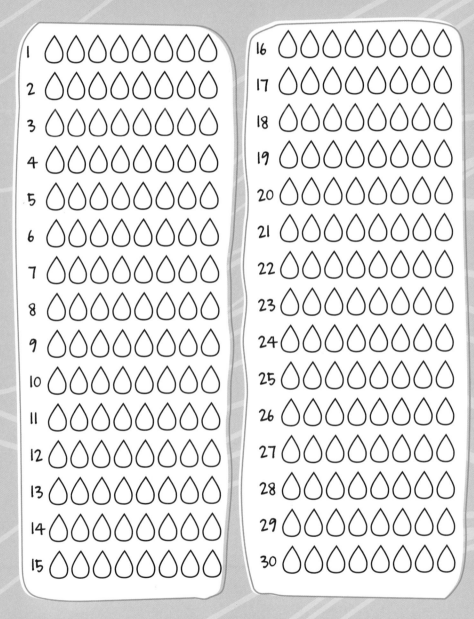

Five-a-Day Tracker

Each apple = one of your five
fruits or vegetables a day

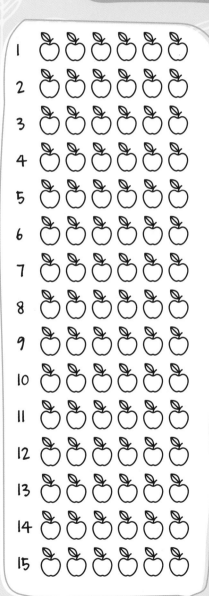

1							16					
2							17					
3							18					
4							19					
5							20					
6							21					
7							22					
8							23					
9							24					
10							25					
11							26					
12							27					
13							28					
14							29					
15							30					

Sleep Tracker

On each day this month, colour in one shape according to how many hours of sleep you had.

KEY

- ◯ Four hours or fewer
- ◯ Five hours
- ◯ Six hours
- ◯ Seven hours
- ◯ Eight hours
- ◯ Nine hours or more

Top Tips

THE SOUND OF SILENCE

It doesn't have to be an expensive retreat that requires you to keep schtum for a week, but the benefits of a bit of quiet time should never be underestimated. Remember at school when the teacher would savvily crack out a game of Sleeping Lions right after everyone had got a little over-excited, and – crucially – just before exhilaration turned to sensory overload and tears? We are still those self-same little beasts, overwhelmed by too much noise or activity, and there's a whole lot of that in adult life, isn't there?

Some people, especially city dwellers, tend to find complete silence a little uncomfortable, but making peace with it – equally, not having high expectations of it – can bring about all sorts of revelations. It can increase our self-compassion, improve our listening skills, help us see truth and work out what's wrong, and provide an often all-important space between a feeling and a knee-jerk response.

We only
ever have the
present moment
to work with

I'm
grateful
for...

Write one thing
that you are
grateful for
each day
this month.

2 3 4 5 6 7 8 9 10 11 12 13 14 15 16 17 18 19 20 21 22 23 24 25 26 27 28 29 30

137

Wellness Tracker

On each day this month, colour in one shape
according to how you feel.

KEY ◯ Great ◯ Good ◯ Average ◯ Poor ◯ Terrible

Happiness is a
form of courage.

HOLBROOK JACKSON

Monthly Goals Tracker

Use this page to write down some of the things that you would like to achieve this month. Then think about ways you could accomplish them, and write down some ideas you could try.

My goal(s) for this month:

Example goal: Increase my activity levels

....

....

....

....

How I can reach them:

Example steps: Use a pedometer to track my steps or join a yoga class

....

....

....

....

Top Tips

HAPPINESS IS NOT LINEAR

People talk about life's ups and downs, and what this really means is that happiness is not to be found at the end of a long, straight road. It's not about racing toward some sort of utopian end goal where everything in our lives is perfect and we are overflowing with peace and wisdom. We never stop learning. Happiness will present at different points – sometimes only very small amounts of it, sometimes in a big wave. Often it shows itself immediately before or after a period of sadness, surprising you when a major life event has knocked you off your feet and you've solemnly declared that you'll never be happy again. Suffering is a part of life, and coming to terms with this needn't make your approach to life any less upbeat. Lows, trying as they are, can enhance highs, so hold on, let yourself feel what you feel, and believe that change will inevitably come.

Self-Care Bucket List

It's important to include a few moments of self-care into every day. By trying just one of these simple self-care activities each week you will enrich your life and nourish your mind, body and soul.

Put on your favourite seasonal songs

Mull a pan of wine with fruits and spices

Decorate your home for the holiday season

Make some chutney, truffles or fudge to give as gifts

Water Tracker

One drop = one glass (400 ml)

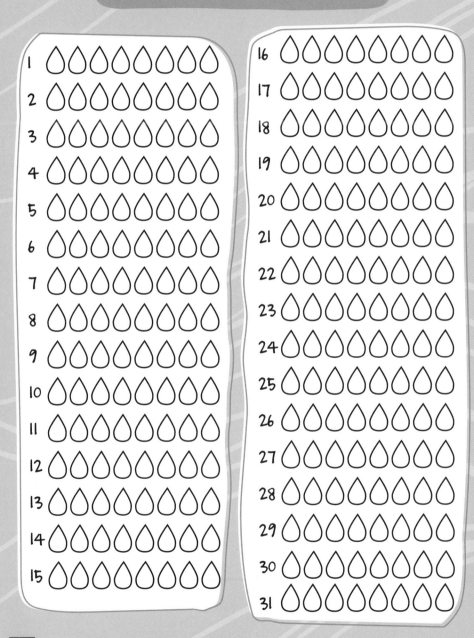

Five-a-Day Tracker

Each apple = one of your five
fruits or vegetables a day

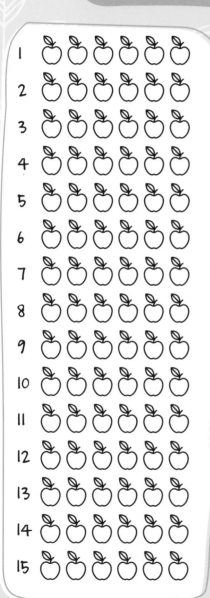

Sleep Tracker

On each day this month, colour in one shape according to how many hours of sleep you had.

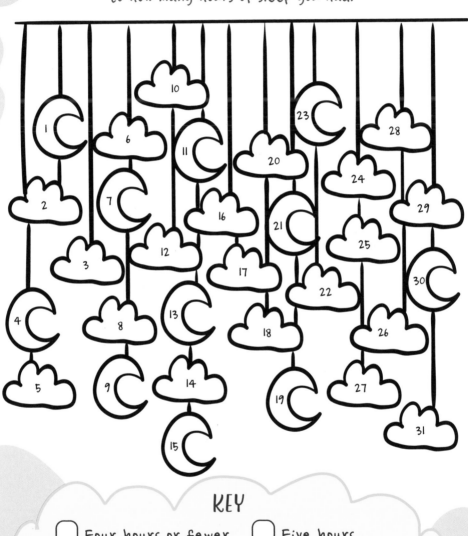

KEY

- ◯ Four hours or fewer
- ◯ Five hours
- ◯ Six hours
- ◯ Seven hours
- ◯ Eight hours
- ◯ Nine hours or more

Top Tips

THE END-OF-YEAR MENTAL STOCK-TAKE

It's time to reflect on what you've achieved – big or small. What went well? What didn't? What did you learn that you can take with you into the next 12 months?

Try to tie up loose ends to avoid starting the new year feeling like you have unfinished business. At the same time, be realistic: don't bite off more than you can chew to meet end-of-year deadlines. December tends to be busy and social demands jostle for your attention with everything else.

What are you finding most stressful? Work out what you can swerve. Stop with the people-pleasing "should" – delete the word from your vocabulary and practise your new-found "no". You needn't accept every invitation just because you're available. Pleasing yourself has benefits for everyone: you'll be all the merrier when you do make an appearance.

Thank those who have supported you, telling them why you love them and congratulating them on their successes, and look forward to the next chapter with a manageable list of things you'd like to do, see, change or try.

You are
enough

I'm grateful for...

Write one thing that you are grateful for each day this month.

2 3 4 5 6 7 8 9 10 11 12 13 14 15 16 17 18 19 20 21 22 23 24 25 26 27 28 29 30 3

149

Conclusion

What's the biggest takeaway here? With any luck, it's the understanding that the enigma that is happiness, when unravelled, means something a little different to everybody. It's inevitable when you think about it – we're all beautifully individual, with our own unique genetic make-up, look, quirks, interests, attractions, personality, potential and pathway.

Being honest with yourself about what you really want, and accepting that your drives and motivations may be different from those you compare yourself to, is a huge accomplishment that takes work. Speaking to ourselves with the same kindness we shower over our best friends can mean years of unpicking the stitches of our tightly sewn seams. If you've not made as much progress this year as you might have hoped, don't be hard on yourself. Remember happiness is not linear, and call to mind the times that joy has materialized throughout the year.

You've tracked your progress, in terms of the more tangible tick boxes, to give yourself the best chance of contentment day-to-day – eating well, staying hydrated and getting good-quality sleep. You've got to grips with goal-setting and gratitude-documenting, thought about the importance of work–life balance, nurturing positive and meaningful relationships, connecting with the natural environment and the positive role that it has to play in well-being.

Happiness is about starting small. It's a funny old creature; best not to put too much pressure on it – rather, feed, water and gently nurture it and it will surely grow.

Notes

Use this space to reflect on your
happiness journey so far.

Also Available

MY LIFE TRACKER
ISBN: 978-1-80007-447-7

MY STRESS TRACKER
ISBN: 978-1-78783-533-7

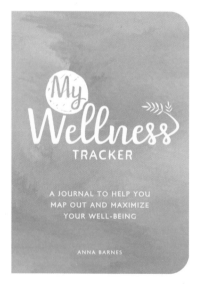

MY WELLNESS TRACKER
ISBN: 978-1-78783-638-9

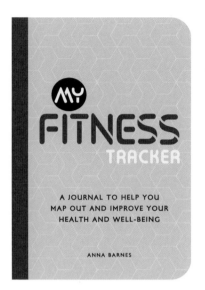

MY FITNESS TRACKER
ISBN: 978-1-80007-448-4

MY SLEEP TRACKER
ISBN: 978-1-78783-532-0

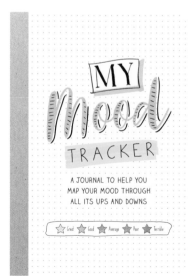

MY MOOD TRACKER
ISBN: 978-1-78783-328-9

Have you enjoyed this book?
If so, why not write a review on your
favourite website?

If you're interested in finding out more
about our books, find us on Facebook
at Summersdale Publishers and follow us
on Twitter at @Summersdale and on Instagram
at @summersdalebooks and get in touch.
We'd love to hear from you!

Thanks very much for buying this
Summersdale book.

www.summersdale.com

Image Credits

Cover images – background © elena_l/Shutterstock.com, flower © SUPRIYANTO
YANTO/Shutterstock.com; pp.3, 4-5, 150-151 – mandalas © Baleika Tamara/
Shutterstock.com; pp.6-7 – sun symbols © ilmeitar/Shutterstock.com; pp.8, 20, 32, 44,
56, 68, 80, 92, 104, 116, 128, 140 – flowers © Irbena/Shutterstock.com; pp.9, 21, 33, 45,
57, 69, 81, 93, 105, 117, 129, 141 – background © sumkinn/Shutterstock.com; pp.10, 15,
22, 27, 34, 39, 46, 51, 58, 63, 70, 75, 82, 87, 94, 99, 106, 111, 118, 123, 130, 135, 142, 147
– dots © Galyna_P/Shutterstock.com; pp.11, 23, 35, 47, 59, 71, 83, 95, 107, 119, 131, 143
– background © Bibadash/Shutterstock.com; pp.12, 24, 36, 48, 60, 72, 84, 96, 108, 120,
132, 144 – background © marukopum/Shutterstock.com; pp.13, 25, 37, 49, 61, 73, 85,
97, 109, 121, 133, 145 – background © adehoidar/Shutterstock.com; pp.16, 28, 40, 52, 64,
76, 88, 100, 112, 124, 136, 148 – circles © pacoillust/Shutterstock.com; pp.18-19 – fruit
symbols © green fox/Shutterstock.com; pp.30-31 – Anna Druzhkova/Shutterstock.com;
pp.42-43 – leaf symbols © leitis/Shutterstock.com; pp.54-55 – kite symbols © sunnyws/
Shutterstock.com, cloud and sun symbols © ANITA'S Studio/Shutterstock.com; pp.66-
67 – shell symbols © Anastasiia_735/Shutterstock.com; pp.78-79 – ice cream symbols ©
frescomovie/Shutterstock.com; pp.90-91 – insect symbols © zabavina/Shutterstock.com;
pp.102-103 – origami symbols © anna42f/Shutterstock.com; pp.114-115 – hot air balloon
symbols © Kamieshkova/Shutterstock.com; pp.126-127 – garland symbols © Zaytseva
Larisa/Shutterstock.com; pp.138-139 – book symbols © In Art/Shutterstock.com